Favorite Bible Verses

This book belongs to

_____

Given by _____ Date _____

Occasion

Tommy NELSON

www.tommynelson.com
A Division of Thomas Nelson, Inc., Nashville, TN
www.ThomasNelson.com

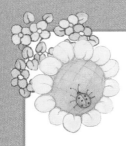

Introduction for Parents

Dear Parents,

Have you ever wanted to share your love of the Bible with your children? Have you wanted to show them how relevant it is to their lives as they experience each day's blessings and challenges? *Precious Moments® Favorite Bible Verses* is the perfect way to introduce your children to God's words of loving, caring, and sharing.

Each section is arranged to help you share with your little one the wisdom of the Bible. The verses are from the International Children's Bible® translation and are accompanied by the endearing illustrations of Sam Butcher's beloved pastel characters. Has your child had a bad day or are they feeling sad? Turn to the section on verses for when they're sad. Do you have trouble

getting them to sleep at bedtime because fear seems to creep into their little heart? Turn to the section on verses for bedtime. Every section includes verses that will soothe, teach, comfort, and encourage.

This beautifully designed book will delight them as they look at the adorable pictures and hear you read aloud the precious words. If they are beginning readers, this translation is just right for them. The International Children's Bible® was created with the understanding level of young children in mind. The words are in large easy-to-read type that will build their confidence as a reader.

We sincerely hope that you and your child enjoy this book and will share many sweet moments together reading and learning God's word.

The Publisher

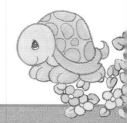

Table of Contents

favorite
Bible
Verses

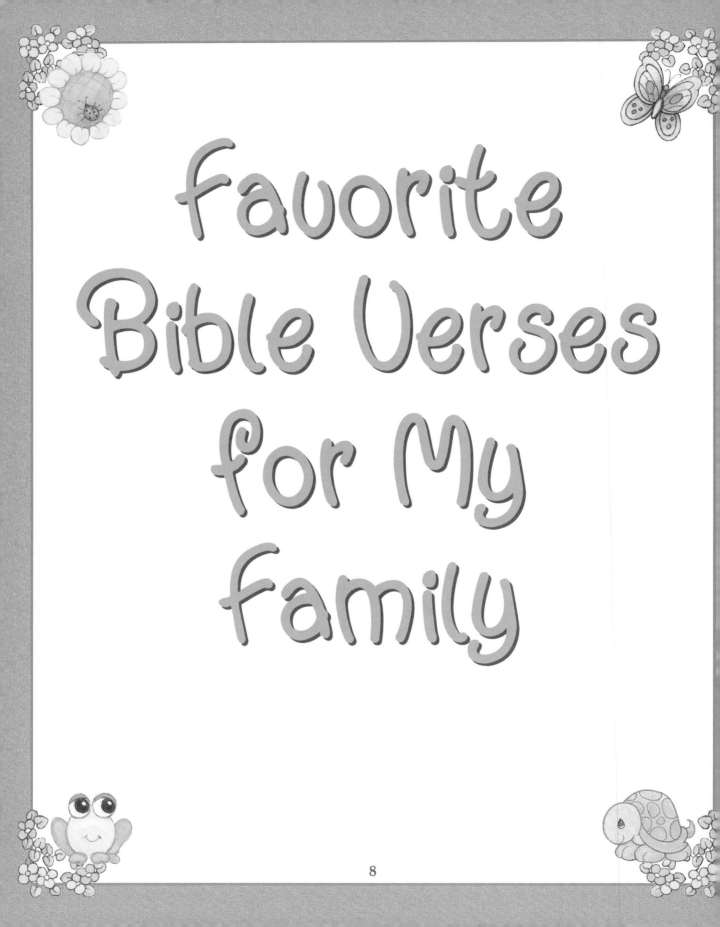

Favorite Bible Verses for My Family

"Honor your father and your mother. The Lord your God has commanded you to do this. Then you will live a long time. And things will go well for you in the land. The Lord your God is going to give you this land."

(Deuteronomy 5:16)

My son, keep your father's commands.

Don't forget your mother's teaching.

Remember their words forever.

Let it be as if they were tied around your neck.

They will guide you when you walk.

They will guard you while you sleep.

They will speak to you when you are awake.

(Proverbs 6:20–22)

Children, obey your parents the way the Lord wants. This is the right thing to do. The command says, "Honor your father and mother." This is the first command that has a promise with it. The promise is: "Then everything will be well with you, and you will have a long life on the earth." (Ephesians 6:1–3)

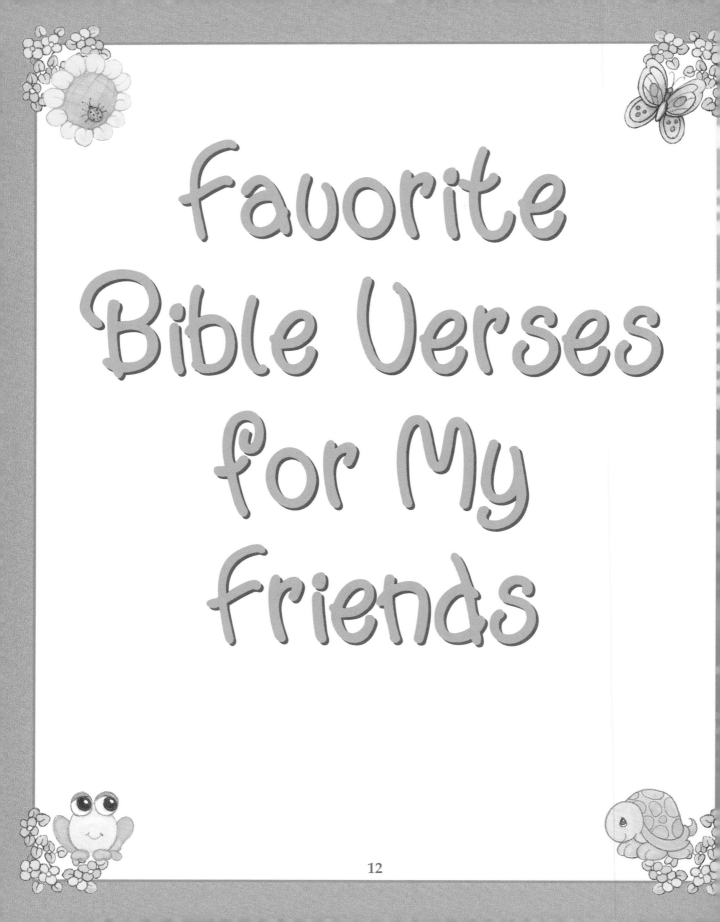

favorite Bible Verses for My friends

A friend loves you all the time.

A brother is always there to help you. (Proverbs 17:17)

"The second most important command is this: 'Love your neighbor as you love yourself.'" (Mark 12:31)

"This is my command: Love each other as I have loved you. The greatest love a person can show is to die for his friends." (John 15:12–13)

No one has ever seen God. But if we love each other, God lives in us. If we love each other, God's love has reached its goal. It is made perfect in us. (1 John 4:12)

Favorite Bible Verses for Faith and Trust

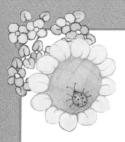

The people who trust the Lord will become strong again.

They will be able to rise up as an eagle in the sky.

They will run without needing rest.

They will walk without becoming tired. (Isaiah 40:31)

Faith means being sure of the things we hope for. And faith means knowing that something is real even if we do not see it. (Hebrews 11:1)

When a person is tempted and still continues strong, he should be happy. After he has proved his faith, God will reward him with life forever. God promised this to all people who love him. (James 1:12)

You have not seen Christ, but still you love him. You cannot see him now, but you believe in him. You are filled with a joy that cannot be explained. And that joy is full of glory. Your faith has a goal, to save your souls. And you are receiving that goal—your salvation. (1 Peter 1:8–9)

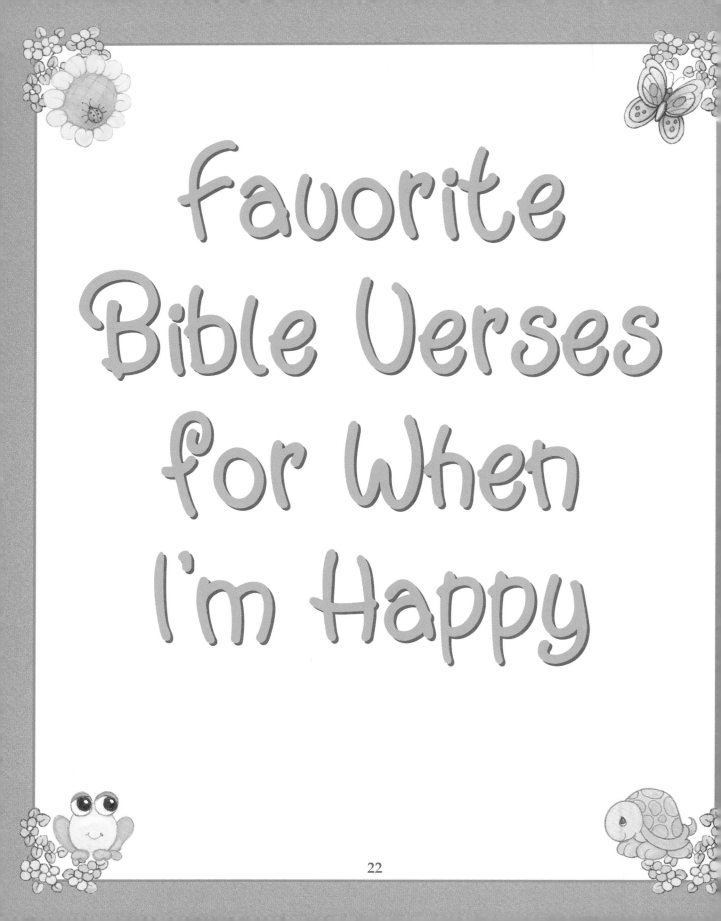

Favorite Bible Verses for When I'm Happy

Everything on earth, shout with joy to God!

Sing about his glory!

Make his praise glorious! (Psalm 66:1–2)

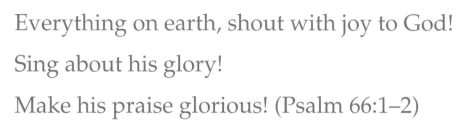

I will praise God in a song.

I will honor him by giving thanks. (Psalm 69:30)

Praise the Lord!

My whole being, praise the Lord.

I will praise the Lord all my life.

I will sing praises to my God as long as I live.

(Psalm 146:1–2)

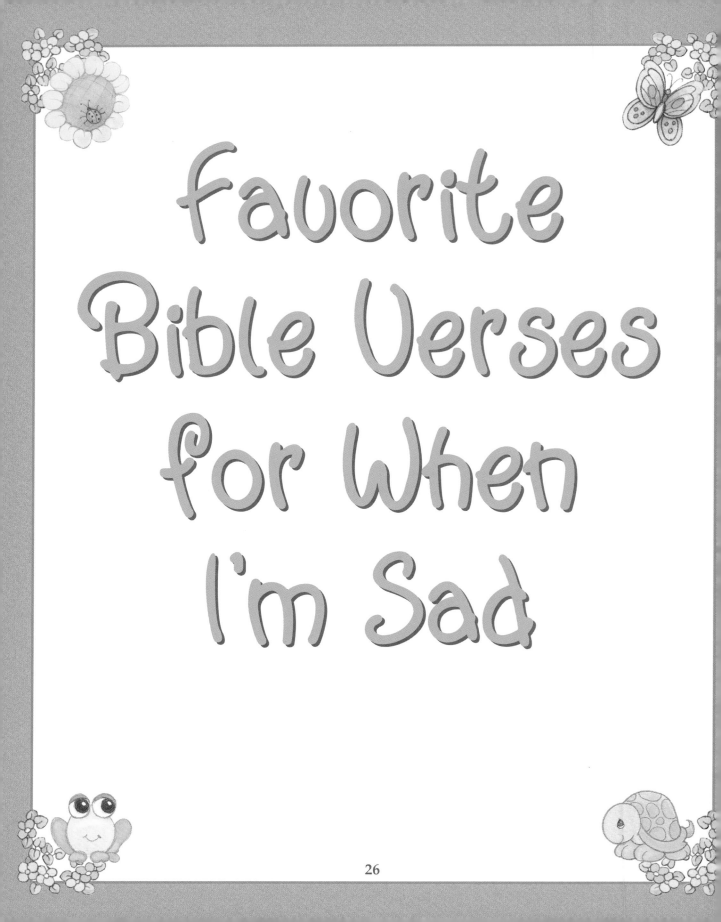

favorite Bible Verses for When I'm Sad

When you pass through the waters, I will be with you.

When you cross rivers, you will not drown.

When you walk through fire, you will not be burned.

The flames will not hurt you. (Isaiah 43:2)

Those who are sad now are happy.

God will comfort them. (Matthew 5:4)

We share in the many sufferings of Christ. In the same way, much comfort comes to us through Christ. If we have troubles, it is for your comfort and salvation. If we have comfort, then you also have comfort. This helps you to accept patiently the same sufferings that we have.
(2 Corinthians 1:5–6)

We pray that the Lord Jesus Christ himself and God our Father will comfort you and strengthen you in every good thing you do and say. God loved us. Through his grace he gave us a good hope and comfort that continues forever. (2 Thessalonians 2:16–17)

favorite Bible Verses for Bedtime

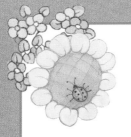

You won't need to be afraid when you lie down.

When you lie down, your sleep will be peaceful.

(Proverbs 3:24)

32

The Lord is good.

He gives protection in times of trouble.

He knows who trusts in him. (Nahum 1:7)

"I leave you peace. My peace I give you. I do not give it to you as the world does. So don't let your hearts be troubled. Don't be afraid." (John 14:27)

I pray that the God who gives hope will fill you with much joy and peace while you trust in him. Then your hope will overflow by the power of the Holy Spirit. (Romans 15:13)

We pray that the Lord of peace will give you peace at all times and in every way. May the Lord be with all of you. (2 Thessalonians 3:16)

Favorite Bible Verses for When I'm Worried or Angry

A gentle answer will calm a person's anger.

But an unkind answer will cause more anger.

(Proverbs 15:1)

Jesus said, "Don't let your hearts be troubled. Trust in God. And trust in me." (John 14:1)

Do not worry about anything. But pray and ask God for everything you need. And when you pray, always give thanks. And God's peace will keep your hearts and minds in Christ Jesus. The peace that God gives is so great that we cannot understand it. (Philippians 4:6–7)

The Lord is faithful. He will give you strength and protect you from the Evil One. . . . We pray that the Lord will lead your hearts into God's love and Christ's patience.
(2 Thessalonians 3:3, 5)

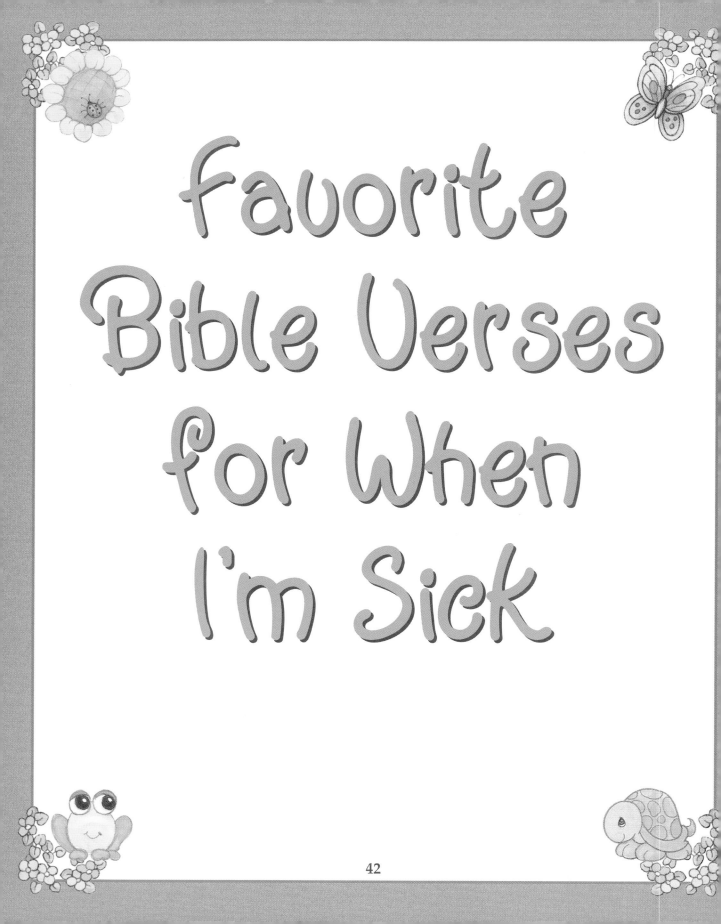

favorite Bible Verses for When I'm Sick

He heals the brokenhearted.

He bandages their wounds. (Psalm 147:3)

Lord, heal me, and I will truly be healed.

Save me, and I will truly be saved.

Lord, you are the one I praise. (Jeremiah 17:14)

The prayer that is said with faith will make the sick person well. The Lord will heal him. And if he has sinned, God will forgive him. (James 5:15)

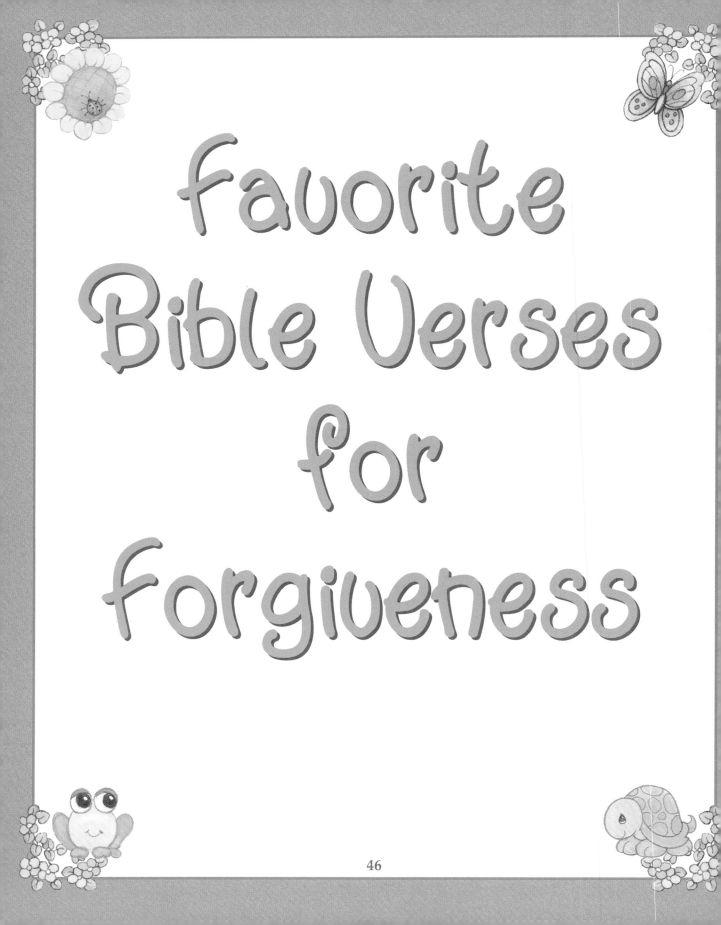

Favorite Bible Verses for Forgiveness

"If you forgive others for the things they do wrong, then your Father in heaven will also forgive you for the things you do wrong. But if you don't forgive the wrongs of others, then your Father in heaven will not forgive the wrong things you do." (Matthew 6:14–15)

"When you are praying, and you remember that you are angry with another person about something, then forgive him. If you do this, then your Father in heaven will also forgive your sins." (Mark 11:25)

Do not be bitter or angry or mad. Never shout angrily or say things to hurt others. Never do anything evil. Be kind and loving to each other. Forgive each other just as God forgave you in Christ. (Ephesians 4:31–32)

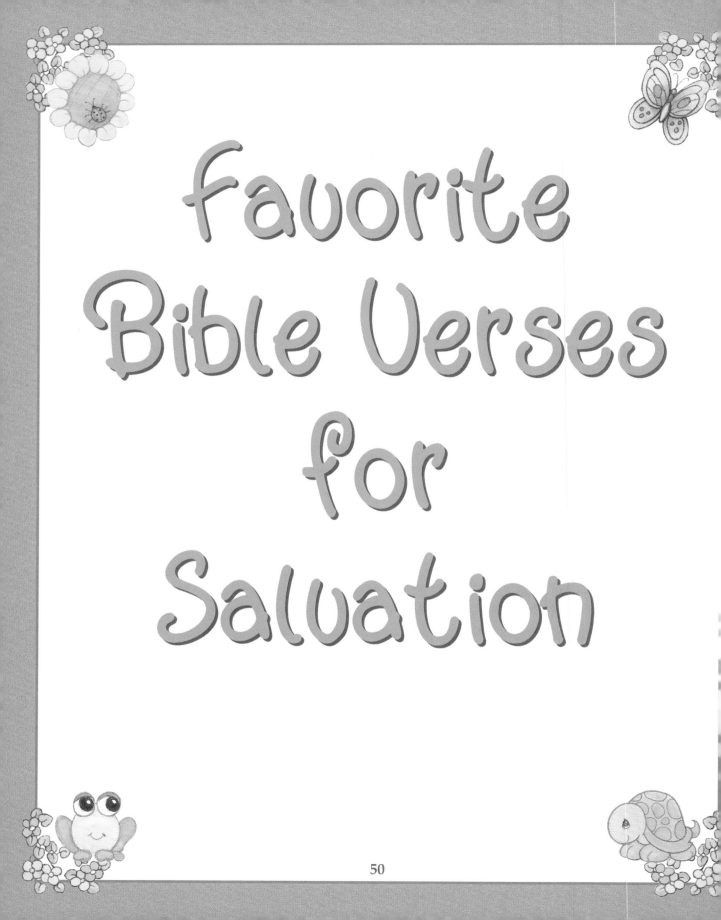

Favorite Bible Verses for Salvation

"If all of you don't change your hearts and lives, then you will be destroyed as they were!" (Luke 13:3)

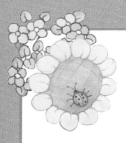

"For God loved the world so much that he gave his only Son. God gave his Son so that whoever believes in him may not be lost, but have eternal life." (John 3:16)

As the Scriptures say: "There is no one without sin. None!"

(Romans 3:10)

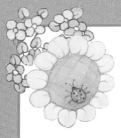

All people have sinned and are not good enough for God's glory. (Romans 3:23)

Christ died for us while we were still sinners. In this way
God shows his great love for us. (Romans 5:8)

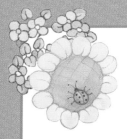

If you use your mouth to say, "Jesus is Lord," and if you believe in your heart that God raised Jesus from death, then you will be saved. We believe with our hearts, and so we are made right with God. And we use our mouths to say that we believe, and so we are saved.

(Romans 10:9–10)

The Scripture says, "Anyone who asks the Lord for help will be saved." (Romans 10:13)

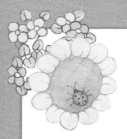

Anyone who does not believe makes God a liar. He does not believe what God told us about his Son. This is what God told us: God has given us eternal life, and this life is in his Son. Whoever has the Son has life. But the person who does not have the Son of God does not have life. (1 John 5:10–12)

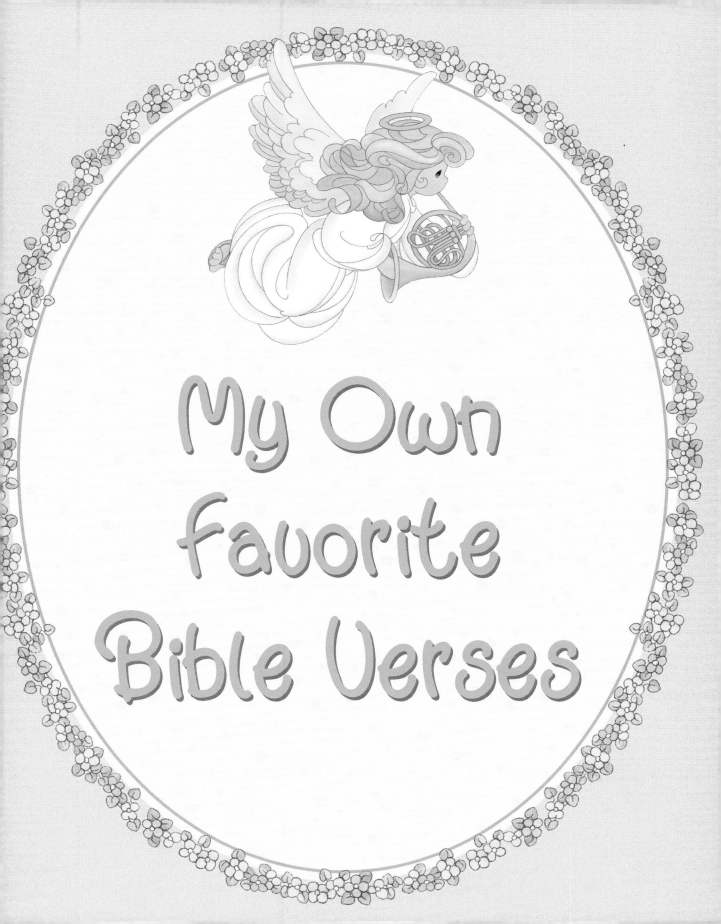

My Own
Favorite
Bible Verses

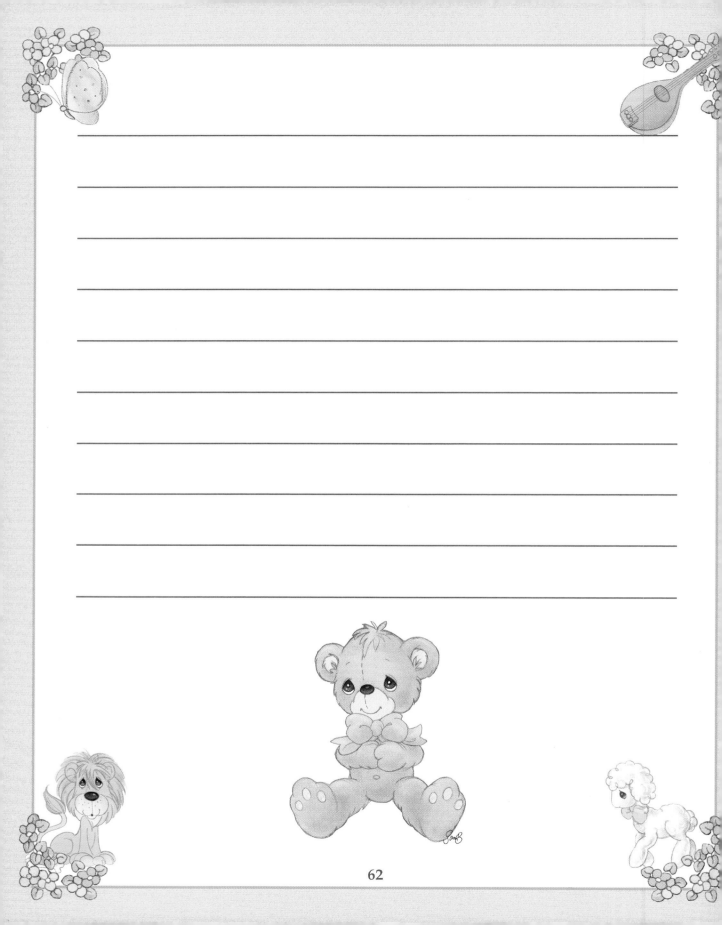